The Mid-Life Crisis Cookbook

by
Gwen Swenson
and
Susan Cunningham

Illustrated by
Mary Engelbreit

Published By
Mid-Lifelines
267 Firestone Drive
Walnut Creek, CA 94598 USA

Copyright © 1982
Gwen Swenson
Susan Cunningham

Illustrations by Mary Engelbreit

First Printing 1980
Second Printing 1982 Revised
Printed in the United States of America

ISBN 0-9609806-1-X Paperback

Appetizers	9
Soups	13
Salads	15
Brunch	17
Vegetables	19
Main Dishes	23
Desserts	29

Introduction

As we are writing this second edition of **The Mid-Life Crisis Cookbook**, we are still trying to explain why we put together the first one. Since journal writing is considered to be good therapy for crisis resolution, we decided to share how this enterprise came to pass.

The original intent of our cookbook was simple (minded) in nature. After years of entering the Publisher's Clearing House Sweepstakes without winning so much as a tote bag, we felt the time had come to take the risk of failing at something on our own merit.

Casting about for a scheme to enrich our lives and provide a cure for two cases of advanced Mid-Life Crisis, we hit upon the idea of selling a collection of our favorite recipes under the snappy title, **46 Success Recipes**.

We sank deeper and deeper into crisis as we began to realize the possibilities for failure were positively stunning. Since the recipes deserved to be shared, we reexamined the title and decided to acknowledge a significant moment in our lives: thus, **The Mid-Life Crisis Cookbook**.

Because so many others shared an appreciation of our condition, we have been able to expand the theme content of our book and present a second edition. (We ought to really have things under control by the 23rd edition.)

The recipes were selected with our "special" audience in mind. They are easy and totally dependable. Many would not be considered everyday fare, but then who needs recipes for boiling hot dogs, frying hamburgers or pouring a bowl of Lucky Charms?

These are recipes which will impress outsiders. After eating these dishes, people genuinely think you are a good cook. That is an especially significant tribute for those of us who think of the kitchen as a cluttered passageway to the larger, more exciting rooms of life.

In conclusion, we'd like to dedicate this book to our families, without whom...enough said.

Mid-Life Crisis Quiz
Am I Having a Mid-Life Crisis?

This quiz is best taken when you are firmly entrenched within the bosom of your family; preferably at a time when each family member was supposed to be somewhere else five minutes ago and dinner is still cooking. Ideally, during this time you may also receive a phone call asking you to bake and decorate two dozen cupcakes for a P.T.A. fundraiser. Taking the quiz under these circumstances will provide you with the definitive answer.

1. You say to your friends, "I think I'm going crazy!" They say in response,
   A. "oh, don't be silly"
   B. "you're so hard on yourself"
   C. "wellllll?...."

2. On the average, you decide you're going to make a significant lifestyle change
   A. annually
   B. monthly
   C. at least daily

3. Your medicine cabinet is filled with
   A. first aid equipment and vitamins
   B. over the counter cold remedies
   C. Stresstabs

4. While reading the newspaper you are naturally drawn to stories about
   A. political issues
   B. self improvement
   C. strange and bizarre tragic events

5. You set out to take care of some necessary business and you are treated shabbily. Your first reaction is to
   A. get angry
   B. assert yourself and resolve the problem
   C. slink home to make Chocolate Chip Cookies and do the wash

6. One of your greatest fantasies is to
    A. have laundry care labels alphabetized in a handy file box
    B. win the Pillsbury Bake-Off
    C. embark on a spiritual quest to Sri Lanka

7. You enroll in a pottery class only to find that you
    A. have previously unrecognized talent
    B. make great ashtrays
    C. can't center the clay

8. You get some of your best ideas
    A. while carefully considering your family's needs
    B. from the "Ask Heloise" column
    C. while cleaning the bathroom

9. The newest addition to your wardrobe is
    A. a pink netted cocktail gown
    B. a pair of Sperry Top-Siders
    C. a T-shirt emblazoned with "Born To Be Wild"

10. When your daughter's handsome date arrives, you
    A. call her
    B. think—"I hope he's a nice boy"
    C. begin to wonder what would happen if she suddenly "took ill" and you **had** to go in her place

Score:
    5 points for C answers   _____
    3 points for B answers   _____
    1 point for A answers   _____
          TOTAL   _____

50—40   You are!
40—30   Marginal. No harm in getting the number of a good therapist.
30—20   Still functioning; but don't misplace this book.
20—10   Try the "Evil Brownies" anyway.

7

Glossary

Beat	a common condition at the end of any given day
Blanch	reaction to hearing that your best friend is expecting her fifth baby
Coddle	a forty minute bath
Dough	a green substance that could make all the difference in the world
Frizzle	coming off a frenzy (See whip)
Glaze	a look in the eyes; particularly recognizable in those who are having a mystical experience or in those who have recently returned from a family vacation
Junket	alternative to mending, cleaning, sorting or recycling
Knead	desire not fulfilled in your current reality based situation
Lard	adipose tissue attached to a formerly firm body structure
Puree	a condition of the spirit if no longer the flesh
Relish	time alone
Roux	sensitivity to the reality of how one spends one's time, as in "I roux the day..."
Scramble	behavior pattern of Super Mothers
Shred	the rending of garments in times of stress
Skim	the diversion of grocery money to pay the fee to have your "colors" done
Steep	the price you pay for independence
Stock	the taking of which may be hazardous to your health
Whip	necessary state preceding a frenzy

Shrimp Mousse

1 can tomato soup
1½ pkg. unflavored gelatin
1 8 oz. pkg. cream cheese
1 C. mayonnaise
¾ C. onions, chopped
¾ C. celery, chopped
½ lb. shrimp, chopped

Heat can of tomato soup. Soften unflavored gelatin by dissolving in a **small** amount of warm water. Add gelatin to soup, stirring fast to prevent lumps. In blender, mix softened cream cheese and mayonnaise. Add soup to mixture and blend. Pour in bowl and add onions, celery and shrimp. Mix with spoon. Put in 1½ qt. greased mold. Chill several hours or overnight. Unmold and serve with crackers.
A variation: substitute cream of mushroom soup, clams or crabmeat and ¼ C. chopped green onions.

Stuffed Mushrooms

1 pkg. Stouffer's frozen Spinach Souffle
2 lbs. large mushrooms
1 C. grated Jack cheese
2 green onions, chopped fine
Parmesan cheese, grated

Thaw Spinach Souffle. Remove stems and clean mushrooms. Mix souffle with Jack cheese and green onions. Stuff the mushrooms with spinach mixture. Sprinkle with the Parmesan cheese. Bake at 350 degrees for 20 minutes.

Red Pepper Jelly

11 C. sweet red bell peppers
    (approximately 24 peppers or 10 lbs.)
4 C. vinegar
6 C. sugar
2 T. non-iodized salt

Rinse and chop peppers into eighths. Remove any white membrane. Finely chop in blender or food processor. Drain. Add salt and allow to drain for at least 2 hours. Squeeze and drain well. Discard juice. Combine vinegar and sugar. Cook a few minutes to form a syrup. Add peppers. Cook over medium heat for approximately ½ hour, until thickened. Stir frequently. Pour into sterilized jars and seal. To serve: spoon generously over block of softened cream cheese. Spread on crackers. Yield: 4-5 pints or 8-10 half pints.

Perfect Clam Dip

8 oz. pkg. cream cheese
1 can minced clams
1½ t. worcestershire sauce
1 T. mayonnaise
1 clove garlic, minced
sour cream, as needed

Combine all ingredients except clams. Beat until smooth (great in food processor). Add clams and as much sour cream as needed for desired consistency. Serve with crackers or potato chips.

Sesame Chicken Wings

A good main dish when used with additional chicken parts.

2½ lbs. chicken wings
1 egg
1 T. water
½ C. flour
¼ C. seasoned breadcrumbs

¼ C. sesame seeds
1 t. salt
¼ t. pepper
1 stick butter

Mix egg and water. Dip wings in egg mixture, then dip into mixture of flour, breadcrumbs, sesame seeds, salt and pepper. Melt stick of butter in 9 x 13 inch baking dish or cookie sheet. Place chicken in dish and bake at 350 degrees for 1 hour or until pieces are browned and crisp.

Chili-Cheese Spread

Grate or Grind:
1 lb. sharp Cheddar cheese
6 hard boiled eggs
3 or 4 green chilies
1 onion

Add:
1 can chopped olives
1 can tomato sauce (8 oz.)
1 t. celery salt
½ t. worcestershire sauce
¼ lb. melted butter
garlic salt to taste

Spread on cocktail rye rounds and broil until cheese mixture is bubbly and lightly browned. Spread on French bread or rye bread and broil for open faced sandwiches. This freezes well.

Layered Nacho Dip

1st layer Mix well	2-15 oz. cans refried beans 1 pkg. Taco Seasoning (Lawry's)
2nd layer Mix well	1 avocado, chopped (or 1 can Avocado Dip) 3 or 4 T. sour cream lemon juice
3rd layer Mix well	2 small cans diced green chiles 2 small cans chopped olives green onions, chopped
4th layer	tomato, chopped cheese, grated (Jack or Cheddar)

Layer in a large serving dish (approximately 9 x 12). Serve cold with tortilla chips. To serve hot, heat through then add tomato and avocado. This can be the stuffing for Burritos or is an excellent base for Tostados.

Rondele

¼ C. cold butter (cut in 3 pieces)
1 small clove garlic
1 pkg. cream cheese, 8 oz. (cut in 6 pieces)
¼ C. fresh parsley leaves
½ t. salt
cracked peppercorns

Process butter and garlic until garlic is finely chopped (30 sec.). Add remaining ingredients and process until parsley is minced. Put in bowl and sprinkle cracked peppercorns over top. Cover and chill until firm. Serve on crackers.

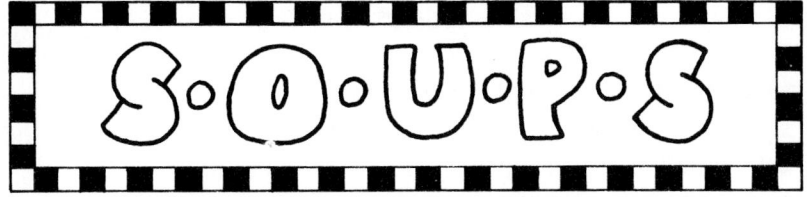

Boston Clam Chowder

½ lb. salt pork, diced
1 large onion, chopped
2½ C. cold water
4 C. red potatoes, diced
3 cans chopped clams

2 C. half and half
1/8 t. thyme
salt, to taste
pepper, to taste
2 T. butter, soft

Fry salt pork in heavy 4 qt. saucepan, stirring constantly for about 3 minutes. Add onion and cook together until both are lightly browned, about 5 minutes. Add water and diced potatoes, bring to a boil then reduce heat and simmer with the pan half covered for 15 minutes or until the potatoes are tender. Add clams, draining 1 can only, juice from the other 2 cans, and thyme. Heat almost to boiling. Taste and season with salt and pepper. Stir in soft butter. Serves 6-8.

Cream of Watercress Soup

2 bunches watercress
1 lb. potatoes
3 T. butter
2 C. chicken broth

1 C. half and half
salt
pepper

Rinse and remove stems from watercress. Cook in small amount of water until limp. Drain. Peel and cube potatoes. Cook in about an inch of water until tender. Puree both potatoes and watercress in blender or food processor until very smooth. Combine all ingredients with seasonings, using broth to thin to desired consistency. Bring to a boil. Serves 4.

Winter Soup

1 large bunch broccoli
1 onion, chopped
2 C. chicken broth
1½ C. half and half
salt
pepper
curry (optional)

Cook broccoli and onion in chicken broth until broccoli is tender. Place all in food processor or blender and whirl until mixture is smooth. Return to saucepan and add cream. Season to taste with salt and pepper. Add curry if desired. Heat but do not boil.
A variation: for a low calorie soup, replace cream with evaporated non-fat or low-fat milk. You may also substitute asparagus or cauliflower for broccoli.

Tortilla Soup

1 quart chicken broth
1 can green chili salsa
½ lb. Jack cheese, grated
Queso Fresco cheese, cubed (soft white Mexican cheese)
    (other variety or Jack cheese may also be used)
1 or 2 avocados, cubed
corn tortillas, crisply fried and broken up

Simmer together the chicken broth and chili salsa. When ready to serve, put handful of Jack cheese in soup bowls and pour in broth. Top with tortilla chips, avocado and Queso Fresco cheese. Serve with lime wedge and rolls.

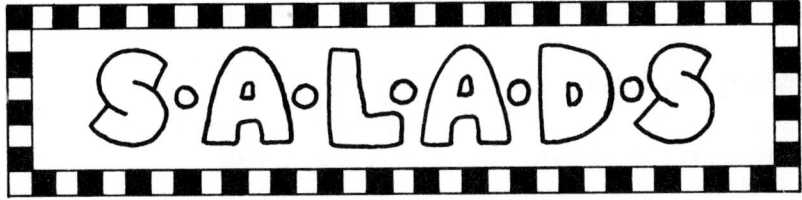

Spinach Salad

3 bunches spinach
¼ C. plus 2 T. wine vinegar
¾ C. salad oil
1 t. Dijon mustard
4 t. chives, chopped
¼ C. green onions, chopped

½ t. salt
¼ t. pepper
2 T. sugar
3 eggs, hard boiled, large chopped
8 slices bacon, crumbled

Wash, drain and refrigerate spinach. Combine vinegar, oil, mustard, chives, green onion, salt, pepper and sugar. Mix well. Tear spinach leaves, add bacon and eggs. Toss with dressing. Serves 6-8.

Mustard Ring

We know this sounds unusual, but it really is good and will do wonders for a baked ham dinner.

4 eggs
¾ C. sugar
1 T. unflavored gelatin
1½ T. dry mustard
½ t. tumeric

¼ t. salt
1 C. water
½ C. cider vinegar
½ pint whipping cream

Beat eggs in top of double boiler. Mix sugar and gelatin together. Add spices, water and vinegar to eggs. Stir in sugar mixture. Cook over boiling water until slightly thickened. Stir constantly. Cool until thick. Whip cream and stir into cooled mixture. Turn into 1½ qt. ring mold (greased). Refrigerate until firm. To serve: unmold and fill center with cole slaw or fresh fruit.

Chinese Green Salad

Iceberg lettuce, shredded
2 C. fresh bean sprouts
½ C. celery, chopped
2 T. green onion, minced
1 can water chestnuts,
    drained and sliced
½ lb. fresh cooked shrimp
    (or 1 can shrimp 6½ oz.)

Dressing:
½ C. mayonnaise
1 t. soy sauce
½ t. curry powder

Combine salad ingredients and toss with dressing. This can be a main dish salad by increasing the amount of shrimp and decreasing the amount of shredded lettuce. Serves 6.

Layered Salad

1 head Iceberg lettuce, shredded
4 green onions, sliced
1 8 oz. can water chestnuts, sliced
½ red or green bell pepper, sliced
2 stalks celery, sliced
1 pkg. frozen peas

2 C. mayonnaise
2 t. sugar
½ C. Parmesan cheese, grated
1 t. salt
¼ t. garlic powder
¾ lb. bacon, fried and drained
3 hard cooked eggs, chopped
2 tomatoes

Spread the lettuce over the bottom of a wide 4 quart serving dish (glass salad bowl looks great). Sprinkle a layer of green onions over lettuce. Add layers of water chestnuts, bell pepper, celery and finish with frozen peas. Spread mayonnaise evenly over peas. Sprinkle with sugar, Parmesan cheese, salt, and garlic powder. Crumble bacon on top, then sprinkle with chopped egg. Cover and chill for 4 hours or as long as 24 hours. When ready to serve, cut tomato in wedges and arrange on top of salad. To serve: use a spoon and fork to lift out each serving, which should include some of each layer. Makes 8-10 servings.

Strata

9 slices bread, cubed
6 eggs
3 C. milk
¾ lb. cheese, grated
¾ T. mustard
¾ t. salt
1 t. worcestershire sauce

Butter large baking dish. Trim crusts from bread and cube. Place bread cubes, grated cheese and any additional ingredients (shrimp, mushrooms, ham slices, chives...your choice) in baking dish. Beat rest of ingredients together and pour over all. Refrigerate several hours or overnight. Bake at 350 degrees for 1 hour.

Eggs and Crab

3 T. butter
8 eggs
2 T. sour cream
3 T. dry vermouth (optional)
½ t. salt
1 C. crabmeat
½ C. shrimp, cooked, shelled and deveined
1 avocado, small chunks

Melt butter in non-stick skillet. Blend sour cream, vermouth and salt. Beat in eggs. Pour egg mixture into sizzling butter and cook, stirring gently. When eggs are a little over halfway set, add shellfish and avocado. Cook until eggs are set. Serves 4.

Artichoke Fritata

2 jars marinated artichoke hearts, drained and chopped
1 small onion, chopped
1 clove garlic, minced
8 eggs, beaten
½ t. salt
½ t. pepper

½ t. oregano
½ t. Tabasco Sauce
2 T. parsley, minced
¼ C. bread crumbs
8 oz. sharp Cheddar cheese grated

Drain 1 jar of the artichoke marinade into a frying pan. Saute onions and garlic in the marinade. Drain artichokes and chop; add to garlic and onions. Saute until onions are golden. Remove from heat. In a large bowl beat eggs. Add onions, garlic and artichokes to the eggs. Mix well. Add spices, bread crumbs and cheese to mixture and mix well. Pour into a greased 7 x 11 inch pan. Bake at 350 degrees for 30 minutes. Cut into 1 inch squares. Serve hot or cold. May also be used as an appetizer.

German Pancakes

6 eggs
1 C. flour

1 t. salt
1½ C. milk

In hot oven, melt 2 T. butter in each of 2 glass pie pans. Beat ingredients in blender until bubbles start to rise. Pour batter in pans and bake in 450-475 degree oven for 15 minutes. Turn oven to 350 degrees and bake for 5 minutes more. Pancakes will be very high and puffy. Cut into wedges and serve hot with sour cream and jam or jelly.
A variation: add ½ t. or more (to taste) of nutmeg to batter. Serve with lemon wedges and powdered sugar.

Best Baked Beans

1 16 oz. can dark red kidney beans, drained
1 16 oz. can light red kidney beans, drained
1 16 oz. can baked pork and beans
½ C. catsup
1 T. dry mustard (mixed with small amount of water)
2 T. brown sugar
2 T. wine vinegar
3 T. white vinegar
6 slices bacon
1 medium onion (red), chopped
1 clove garlic, minced
1 or 2 whole cloves
1 t. parsley, chopped

Fry bacon until crisp. Remove from skillet and reserve. Saute chopped onion and garlic in bacon drippings. Mix together catsup, dissolved mustard, brown sugar, vinegar, wine vinegar, parsley and cloves. Add to onions in skillet and simmer partially covered for 5 to 10 minutes. Empty all beans into casserole and add rest of mixture. Crumble bacon on top and bake (covered) at 350 degrees for 1 hour.

Ratatouille Nicoise

1 eggplant
2 zucchini
6 tomatoes
4 T. olive oil
1 onion, chopped

1 clove garlic, minced
1 T. parsley, chopped
1 bay leaf
salt and pepper
½ C. grated Parmesan cheese

Peel and cube eggplant and zucchini. Peel tomatoes and cut into wedges. Heat olive oil in large skillet. Saute onion until brown. Add minced garlic, parsley, bay leaf, eggplant, zucchini, salt and pepper to taste. Saute approximately 20 minutes. Add tomatoes and cook a few more minutes. Move to a shallow baking dish. Sprinkle with cheese and brown under broiler. Serves 6-8.

California Spinach

3 pkgs. frozen chopped spinach
½ pint sour cream
1 pkg. Lipton Onion Soup Mix

½ t. salt
nutmeg

Cook and drain spinach. Combine rest of ingredients with spinach. Place in buttered casserole. Top with nutmeg. Bake uncovered at 325 degrees for 20 minutes. Serves 6.

Barley Casserole

1 C. barley (wash and rinse)
½ C. pine nuts
   (or sliced almonds)
4 T. butter
½ C. onions, chopped

¼ C. green onions, chopped
¼ C. parsley, chopped
¼ t. salt
¼ t. pepper
2 cans chicken broth (28 oz.)

Melt 2 T. butter and lightly toast pine nuts. Remove from heat. Add 2 T. butter and brown barley and onions. Add green onions, parsley, salt and pepper. Heat chicken broth. Add to mixture. Mix well. Place in buttered casserole. Bake uncovered at 375 degrees for 1 hour and 10 minutes. Serves 6.

Cheddar Potatoes

6 medium potatoes
2 C. Cheddar cheese, grated
2 C. sour cream
⅓ C. butter

⅓ C. green onion, chopped
1 t. salt
½ t. pepper

Parboil, cool and grate potatoes. Cook last six ingredients until cheese is melted. Mix with potatoes in 2 qt. buttered casserole. Dot top with butter. Bake in 325 degree oven for 25 minutes. Serves 6.

Broccoli in Clam Sauce

3 10 oz. pkgs. frozen broccoli spears (or 2 bunches fresh broccoli)
1 can Snow's Condensed New England Clam Chowder
½ C. sour cream
½ t. salt
½ C. Cheddar cheese, grated

Prepare frozen broccoli as directed. Drain. Arrange in buttered 9 x 11 inch baking dish. In saucepan, combine clam chowder, sour cream and salt. Cook, stirring until hot. Spoon over broccoli. Bake at 325 degrees for 20 minutes. Remove. Sprinkle with grated cheese. Return to oven until cheese melts. Serves 8.

Broccoli Souffle

1 bunch broccoli
1 onion, chopped
4 T. butter
4 T. flour
1 C. milk

1 t. seasoned salt
3 eggs
½ C. mayonnaise
¼ C. chopped parsley

Cook, drain and chop broccoli. In skillet, saute onion in 4 T. butter. Remove skillet from heat and the flour and milk. Add seasoned salt. Heat to boiling slowly. Beat eggs and add to cream sauce. Combine mayonnaise and parsley with broccoli. Add cream sauce. Pour into well greased casserole. Bake at 350 degrees for 50 to 60 minutes with casserole set in pan of water.

MAIN DISHES

Chicken Wild Rice Casserole

2 whole chickens
1 C. water
1 C. dry sherry
1½ t. salt
½ t. curry powder
1 medium onion, sliced
½ C. celery, sliced

1 lb. mushrooms, sliced
¼ C. butter
2 pkgs. long grain
    and wild rice
1 C. sour cream
1 can cream of
    mushroom soup

Place chicken in deep kettle; add water, sherry, salt, curry, onion and celery. Bring to boil. Cover tightly, reduce heat and simmer 1 hour. Remove from heat, strain broth. Refrigerate chicken and broth at once. When chicken is cooled remove meat from bones, discard skin. Cut into chunks. Saute mushrooms in butter until golden. Cook rice according to package directions, using remaining chicken broth as part of liquid. Combine chicken, rice and mushrooms in 3½ to 4 quart casserole. Blend sour cream and undiluted soup. Toss together with chicken mixture. Heat covered in 350 degree oven 1 hour. Serves 8-10.

This recipe is easier if you cook and bone the chicken the night before. Combine ingredients beforehand and all you have to do is bake and serve. Recipe doubles well.

Marinated Flank Steak

This is excellent accompanied by the Cheddar Potatoes and Spinach Salad.

Teriyaki Marinade:
¾ C. salad oil
¼ C. soy sauce
¼ C. honey

2 T. wine vinegar
1 clove garlic, minced
2 T. green onion, chopped
1½ t. ground ginger

Mix all ingredients. Pour over Flank Steak and marinate overnight or at least 2 hours. The longer the better! Barbeque or broil to desired doneness. Slice meat on the diagonal and serve. This marinade may also be used with chicken parts, spareribs, shish kebobs and fish.

Veal Marsala

1½ lbs. veal scallops, sliced 3/8 inch thick, pounded to ¼ inch thick
salt
pepper
flour

2 T. butter
3 T. olive oil
½ lb. fresh mushrooms, sliced
½ C. dry Marsala wine
½ C. chicken or beef broth
2 T. fresh parsley, minced

Season veal with salt and pepper, dip in flour and shake off excess. Melt butter and olive oil in heavy skillet. Saute veal until browned, about 3 minutes per side. Remove veal. Saute mushrooms (add more butter if necessary), add wine and stock and boil briskly for a few minutes, scraping any browned bits from skillet. Return veal to pan, cover and simmer over low heat 10-15 minutes. To serve: remove veal to heated platter, boil sauce until it has reduced considerably and has the consistency of a syrupy glaze. Pour sauce over veal and sprinkle with fresh parsley. Serves 4.

Scampi

1½ C. onions, chopped
½ C. butter
3 lbs. fresh shrimp
   (shelled and deveined)
½ C. oil
½ C. parsley, chopped

3-5 cloves garlic, crushed
2 T. lemon juice
1½ t. salt
¾ t. pepper

Saute onions in butter until limp. Pour into large bowl. Add shrimp, oil, parsley, garlic, lemon juice, salt and pepper. Toss together. At this point you may cover and refrigerate until ready to cook. Spread shrimp and sauce in a single layer on a pan with a small lip. Broil 3-5 minutes, 6 inches from the fire. Turn and do the same on the second side. This is nice served on steamed rice. Serves 6.

Scallops Saute Provencial

1½ lbs. scallops
seasoned flour
   (salt, pepper, paprika)
3 T. olive oil
1-2 cloves garlic, minced

¼ C. white wine
½ C. fresh parsley, chopped
salt and pepper

Dust scallops with flour. Heat oil, add scallops and garlic. Cook quickly (5 minutes). Add wine, salt and pepper. Cook a few minutes or until wine is reduced and scallops are firm. Remove from heat and toss with parsley. Do not overcook scallops. Serves 4.

Shellfish Sauce

1 C. mayonnaise
3 T. baby food spinach
½ t. onion powder

1½ T. Tarragon vinegar
1 T. chervil

Combine mayonnaise, spinach, onion powder, vinegar and chervil. Chill. Serve with cold shellfish. Especially good with cracked crab.

Sweet and Sour Beef Stew

¼ C. flour
2 t. salt
¼ t. pepper
2 lbs. beef stew meat in 1" cubes
2 T. salad oil
½ C. catsup
¼ C. brown sugar, packed

¼ C. wine vinegar
1 T. worcestershire sauce
1 C. water
1 large onion, chopped
4 carrots, chopped
egg noodles (optional)
parsley, chopped (optional)

Combine flour, 1 t. salt and pepper. Coat meat with flour. In heavy Dutch oven, brown meat in oil. Drain excess fat. Combine catsup, brown sugar, vinegar, worcestershire, water and remaining 1 t. salt; pour over meat and add onion. Cover pan, reduce heat and simmer for 1 hour and 15 minutes. Stir occasionally. Add carrots and cook until meat and carrots are tender, about 40 minutes. Serve alone or over noodles. Garnish with parsley. If you don't use noodles, you may add quartered potatoes when you add carrots. Serves 4-6.

Artichoke Chicken Rosé

6 chicken thighs
3 whole chicken breasts, halved
flour seasoned with salt and pepper
8 T. butter
4 T. flour
1½ C. chicken broth

1 C. rose wine
1 can artichoke hearts
1 bunch green onions, sliced (tops too)
½ lb. mushrooms, sliced and sauteed

Dust chicken pieces with seasoned flour. Melt 4 T. butter in shallow baking dish. Place chicken in single layer, skin side down; bake uncovered in 350 degree oven for 40 minutes. Meanwhile, melt 4 T. butter in saucepan. Stir in flour. Add broth and wine, cook stirring constantly until smooth and thickened. Remove chicken from oven. Turn. Sprinkle with green onions, artichoke hearts and mushrooms. Pour sauce over all. Return to oven, reduce heat to 325 degrees and bake for 25 minutes longer. Serves 6.

Lemon-Pepper Chicken

1 medium chicken fryer, cut up
mayonnaise
cracker crumbs
salt
lemon-pepper seasoning (Lawry's preferred)

Coat chicken pieces with mayonnaise. Sprinkle with salt and lemon-pepper. Roll in cracker crumbs. Place on cookie sheet. Bake at 325 degrees for 1 hour and 15 minutes. Serves 4.

Taco Salad

½ lb. ground beef
1 clove garlic, minced
2 C. kidney beans, drained
1 C. tomato juice

1 t. salt
1 t. cumin
1 t. chili powder
½ t. pepper

Brown ground beef. Drain fat. Combine with rest of ingredients. Simmer 15 minutes.

Mix:
2 C. tortilla chips, crushed
½ head lettuce, shredded
2 tomatoes, chopped
1 avocado, sliced

3 green onions, sliced
1 C. Cheddar cheese, grated
1 C. olives, chopped and drained

Toss hot meat mixture with salad mixture and serve with sour cream or chopped green chilies.

Chilies Quelles

8 flour tortillas
2 C. cooked diced chicken meat
1 can cream of mushroom soup
1 can golden mushroom soup
3 oz. can diced Ortega Green Chilies
½ lb. Jack or Cheddar cheese, grated

Fry tortillas in oil until very crisp. Drain. When cooled, break into 2 inch pieces. Combine with remaining ingredients. Bake in greased casserole at 350 degrees for 20 minutes. Serve on shredded lettuce (sprinkled with wine vinegar). Top with any or all of the following: green onions, tomatoes, olives, avocado and sour cream. Serves 4-6.

New York Cheese Cake

Crust:
½ C. butter, melted
20 squares graham crackers, crushed (1 ¾ C.)
½ t. cinnamon
1 T. sugar

Blend all ingredients. Spread and press into a 9 inch spring form pan, going about 3 inches up sides.

Filling:
3 8 oz. cubes cream cheese, softened
1 C. sugar
4 eggs
2 t. vanilla
¼ t. lemon peel, grated

Beat until smooth and pour into crust. Bake at 350 degrees for 60 minutes or until firm.

Topping:
1 pint sour cream
1 T. sugar
1 t. vanilla

Mix well and ladle on top of cheesecake. Bake at 350 degrees an additional 10 minutes.

Swedish Tea Ring

1 box yellow cake mix
1 large pkg. vanilla pudding
4 eggs
¾ C. oil
¾ C. water
1 t. butter flavoring
1 t. vanilla

Combine all ingredients. Mix well.

Filling:
¼ C. sugar
2 t. cinnamon
¼ C. nuts, chopped

Mix well. Sprinkle filling over batter as you pour it in bundt pan or angel food cake pan, about ⅓ at a time, using batter as last addition. Bake at 350 degrees for 45 to 60 minutes or until done.

Glaze:
1 C. powdered sugar
3 T. milk (or enough to make a glaze that pours)
½ t. vanilla
½ t. butter flavoring

Combine all ingredients and pour over cake while still warm.

Chocolate Hershey Pie

½ C. milk
20 marshmallows
6 Almond Hershey bars

½ pint whipping cream
1 graham cracker crust

Melt marshmallows in milk. Break up Hershey bars in milk and melt. Cool. Whip cream; fold into cooled Hershey mixture. Pour into crust. Chill.

Berry Tart

4-6 C. berries
1½ C. flour (unsifted)
¼ t. baking powder
¼ t. salt
½ C. butter, soft

1 egg
⅓ C. sugar
2 T. flour
¼ C. powdered sugar

Wash and thoroughly drain berries (blueberries, blackberries or raspberries). In bowl combine 1½ C. flour, baking powder, salt, sugar, butter and egg. With hands, work mixture into uniform texture and shape into a ball. Press dough into 11 inch tart pan with removeable bottom. (They are very inexpensive and worth the money for the dramatic results!) Gently stir 2 T. flour into the berries and put into the crust. Bake at 350 degrees for about 50 minutes or until the crust is lightly browned. Cool a bit and remove sides of pan. Sift powdered sugar over top just before serving.

To make a spectacular strawberry tart, make crust (works well in food processor) and bake unfilled until lightly browned, about 20 minutes. Cool crust. Combine 3 small baskets of strawberries with commercially made strawberry glaze. Pour into cooled crust and refrigerate. Serve with whipped cream.

Dessert Topping

1 C. sour cream
½ C. sifted powdered sugar
¼ t. vanilla

1 t. lemon juice
1 t. lemon peel

Combine all ingredients. Stir well. Chill until ready to use. This is a different and delicious alternative to whipped cream. Use on fruit, pie or shortcake.

Raw Apple Cake

2 C. sugar
3 eggs
1¼ C. salad oil
2½ C. flour
½ t. salt

1 t. baking soda
2 t. vanilla
2 t. cinnamon
1 t. nutmeg
4 C. diced apples

Combine sugar and eggs. Beat well. Add oil and cream thoroughly. Sift (optional) flour, soda, salt and spices. Add to egg mixture. Stir in apples. Mix thoroughly. Batter will be thick. Bake about 50 minutes at 350 degrees in a greased 9 x 13 inch pan. Ice with Cream Cheese Frosting.

Cream Cheese Frosting

1 stick butter, softened
1 box powdered sugar

8 oz. cream cheese, softened
2 t. vanilla

Blend all ingredients in mixer until smooth and creamy. Spread on cooled cake.

Lemon Bars

1 C. flour
½ C. butter
¼ C. powdered sugar
2 eggs

1 C. granulated sugar
½ t. baking powder
¼ t. salt
2 T. lemon juice

Blend flour, butter and powdered sugar until mixture just holds together. Press into square pan (8 x 8 x 2). Bake at 350 degrees for 20 minutes. Beat the rest of the ingredients together. Pour over crust and bake an additional 20 to 25 minutes. Do not overbake. Puffs during baking but flattens when cooled. Make 16 squares.

"Evil Brownies"

Brownies:

½ C. butter, softened
1 C. sugar
4 eggs
1 lb. can Hershey's Chocolate Syrup
1 t. vanilla
½ t. salt
1 C. flour

Cream butter and sugar. Add eggs. Stir in syrup, vanilla, salt and flour. Mix well. Bake in 9 x 13 inch pan, 20-25 minutes at 350 degrees.

Frosting:

½ C. butter
¼ C. milk
1 C. sugar
1 C. chocolate chips

Combine in a saucepan, butter, milk and sugar. Boil 30 seconds. Remove from heat. Stir in chocolate chips. Spread on warm brownies. Sprinkle with chopped nuts, if desired. Freezes well.

Krispie Oatmeal Cookies

1 C. shortening
1 C. granulated sugar
1 C. brown sugar
2 eggs
1½ C. flour
2 C. oatmeal
1 t. soda
1 t. salt
1 t. vanilla
1 pkg. chocolate chips

Cream shortening and sugars together. Add eggs. Beat well. Add flour, oatmeal, baking soda, salt and vanilla. Mix well. Stir in chocolate chips. Drop by spoonfuls on cookie sheet. Bake at 350 degrees for 10-12 minutes.

Shortbread

1 ¼ C. flour, unsifted
3 T. cornstarch

¼ C. sugar
½ C. butter, cut in chunks

With your hands, work mixture until it is very crumbly and no large particles remain. Press mixture into a firm lump with your hands. Place dough in a 8 or 9 inch pan with removable bottom (may also use pie pan) and press out firmly until smooth. Impress edge of the dough with the tines of a fork, then prick surface evenly. Bake at 325 degrees for 35 minutes. Remove from oven and while warm cut with a sharp knife into 8-12 wedges. Sprinkle with 1 T. sugar. Let cool.

Rocky Road Candy

1 ½ lb. bulk chocolate
large marshmallows

nuts
butter

Stir and melt chocolate in a double boiler over steaming (not boiling) water. Line sides and bottom of 9 x 13 inch pan with buttered wax paper. Smear bottom of pan with part of the chocolate. Line up the marshmallows side by side. Stick nuts between marshmallows. Spoon chocolate over top, working in between each marshmallow. Pour layer of chocolate on top. Refrigerate to set. Cut into chunks.

Coffee Party

During a Mid-Life Crisis there is the temptation to totally succumb to the ever present feeling of inertia. However...it is occasionally necessary to invite in guests. When we have been confronted with this possibility, rather than getting involved in the cooking of an elaborate meal, and running the real risk of a "nervous spell", we entertain with a coffee party.

Borrow a large coffee maker from a local market (usually free of charge). Buy enough good coffee to allow at least 3 cups per person. (1 cup grounds brews 16 cups of coffee.) We suggest decaffeinated beans ground for the percolator.

Provide an ample amount of whipped cream, chilled in a large bowl of ice. This is the one irresistible ingredient, so be very generous when estimating the quantity.

Copy a variety of coffee recipes, and arrange the cards with all the ingredients on a large serving area so that everyone may help themselves. Guests involved in the creation of their "choice" naturally engage in animated conversation, leaving the hostess free to pursue her private thoughts.

Have a few easy desserts set up in another self-serve area...a favorite cake, cookies and a cheese cake work well.

Cappucino
coffee
whipped cream
sprinkle with:
cinnamon
nutmeg
orange peel

Mexican Fiesta
coffee
cream
cinnamon stick
grated chocolate
Kahlua

Martineque Coffee
coffee
whipped cream
sugar
cinnamon
nutmeg
Rum

Irish Coffee
coffee
whipped cream
Irish Whiskey

Caribbean Coffee
coffee
whipped cream
nutmeg
Rum

Brazilian Cup
coffee
whipped cream
cinnamon stick
grated chocolate
Creme de Cacao

Helpful Hints

This section is designed to be an addendum to a world full of good advise. Consider the hints as potential life savers as you cautiously make your way through the **mind** fields of life.

Menu Planning Plan each day's menu as a whole! Consider your breakfast and lunch when you plan your dinner menu. After all, a cup of coffee, a stale donut and a peanut butter sandwich might play havoc with Nouvelle Cuisine.

Memorable appetizers and an abundance of wine may create a situation in which no one will remember the rest of the meal.

If you only have the time or energy for one homemade dish, make it a good HOT soup. Burnt tongues provide wonderful respite from any potential criticism.

Light salad suppers go particularly well with heavy cholesterol conversation.

Mealtimes Keep mealtime conversations pleasant. It is important for family and friends to relax and enjoy as they eat. It simply will not do to quote from the latest article on Runaway Mothers at the table.

Create effusive centerpieces if you wish to eliminate "meaningful" conversation.

Switch the scene of family meals from time to time. Sometimes serve dinner on trays, perhaps another time at a fireside table, or on a summer evening move outside, pack a picnic and spread out on a blanket on the porch. You might want to try hiding the dinner and watch everyone look for it; or perhaps even having no dinner at all might be a fun change.

For that awkward pause when the roast has been carved and you're surreptitiously taking the peas out of the freezer, suggest 15 minutes of meditation.

Hard Times

Keep an emergency shelf known only to you. It should resemble all the other piles of junk you are always going to sort through; this bit of deception insures that "the shelf" remains personal.

It should include:
—one bottle Excedrin Extra Strength
—newspaper clippings relating to recent studies on the healthful benefits of extra weight
—six pack of Diet Cola
—variety of college catalogs
—one trashy novel; your choice
—recording of "Bridge Over Troubled Waters"
—Sunday's Help Wanted section
—well thumbed copy of **The Cinderella Complex**
—phone numbers of friends home by 4 o'clock
—samples of Law School Aptitude Test
—½ liter dry white wine
—worry beads

Avoidances Minimize stress by avoiding:

Decorating ideas involving empty bleach bottles, cottage cheese cartons, or toilet paper tubes

Direct sales parties

3 x 5 index cards designed to organize your life

Any suggestion of greeting your husband at the door wearing pink "baby dolls" and white majorette boots

Making acid comments when observing your 15 year old watching **Mr. Rogers**

Referring to your two lovely children as "ball" and "chain"

The temptation to respond to the question "and what do you do?"

Acquaintances whose shopping carts are suspiciously nutrition oriented

People who feel that children are the direct product of their environment

Mid-Life Crisis Cookbook
267 Firestone Drive
Walnut Creek, CA 94598

Please send me _____ copies of your cookbook. I am enclosing $4.50 per copy plus $1.00 each for postage and handling.

Name _____

Address _____

City _____ State _____ Zip _____

Mid-Life Crisis Cookbook
267 Firestone Drive
Walnut Creek, CA 94598

Please send me _____ copies of your cookbook. I am enclosing $4.50 per copy plus $1.00 each for postage and handling.

Name _____

Address _____

City _____ State _____ Zip _____

Mid-Life Crisis Cookbook
267 Firestone Drive
Walnut Creek, CA 94598

Please send me _____ copies of your cookbook. I am enclosing $4.50 per copy plus $1.00 each for postage and handling.

Name _____

Address _____

City _____ State _____ Zip _____